Shattered Pieces
Random Slivers in Verse

Emily St. James

Acknowledgments

An enormous thank you to my community of believers who have helped me find who I can be . . . Kerry, Heather, Jill, June, Betsy, Denise, Laura, Lisa, Lori, Risa, Janis, Cindy, and Andrea
Thank you for letting me use your pictures to express myself

When she thought of hell as the inferno of Dante's making, it was less scary. She knew she was playing with fire by committing the sin daily. It was the eternal flames of damnation that she felt when he was near, those promised her by Jonathan Edwards. The thread, the spider's string holding her out of hell, was simply the prayers of her friends. The sin, the temptation, seemed pleasant – it was the warming fire of . . . . life, ok, maybe of desire, and not the sulfurous burn of hell, of the mark of sin. Why was the letter scarlet anyway? Because of the fire, of the flames of hell that beckon the adulteress.

Exordium

*It is the words we choose that create our pasts,
embellish our present,
and determine our future*

You asked me to write a love poem for you – for you?
You asked for the impossible
I write down words without meaning
Love without feeling
It's all I had
You stripped me and left me with only words to cover my nakedness
My soul is bare, exposed and like a transparent eyeball (as he said), even the slightest touch is uncomfortable and undesirable
It is not for you
My soul must fit somewhere
It is not with you
Love must exist
It cannot be a myth, but it is not real here
It is not real with you
The words you say fill my ears
 and spill into my soul
 like a flame thrown from hell
And they are cooled with laughter
 but never with apologies
It is a world without regret or consequence
Where you alone stand high and mighty
So I shut it out and reach to find a smile
It is not with you
I know that forever is a long time to hurt;
it is a long time to care;
a long time to respect;
time to love;
to live;
I know forever
It is not with you

Accusing me again,

you curse and scream

I walk on tiptoes in my own home

I live to please you and continue to be wrong

I watch as the pieces shatter

and splatter the floor

But I cannot pick up my soul every time

It is only my soul

You have been given strength beyond my faith at times

and I cannot win

I cannot continue to fight Satan

in you, from you

We separate. I exist. You exist.

Heaven and Hell

Blending in between

Every day I watch you
hold me,
comfort me,
love me
In my mind
I've written you a thousand love letters
In my mind
You've given me renewed hope
and stronger faith
with kind words and gentle caresses
In my mind

You slam the door and shout at me
for what this time?
You threaten, curse,
lose control again
And I retreat
Going out of my mind

I opened the door

But I could not find it

Every shelf was empty

There was nothing there

    where something once was

I know. Maybe behind all the fear –

No, it's still not there

Maybe if I just move the insensitivity over –

No, it's not there either

If I had the courage, I could look behind disrespect

Or behind selfishness,

Or close-mindedness,

Or aggressiveness,

Or anger,

Or evil

But I am too afraid.

I remain soul-less

Until someone returns it to me

I watch you smile and feel my heart beat

I reach to you, and you're there

Your body melts my soul

And I hunger for your hands touching me

You caress me, and I can't catch my breath

I fall helplessly into your bed

The passion within me grows

Until desire overtakes me, and I pull you closer

Our lips meet and my stomach leaps with pleasure

Your tongue pierces through me, every inch of my skin

I move forward onto you, into you,

Becoming one body, one soul, one desire

One

Where I'm From

I am from books to read,
from cotton fields and muddy irrigation ditches;
I am from papers to grade,
from bulletin board creations with tempra paint mixed from powder.

I am from Grandma's house, with its towering trees inviting us to climb.
I'm from the barracks behind Grandma's house overflowing with old refrigerators and dishwasher racks and broken-down pig pens and chicken coops perfect for playing house.

I'm from crispies and cornflake chicken,
from award-winning lemon pound cake
and coffee- black, please – drunk, with the women buying Avon from Grandma.

I am from MaMa and PaPa and my Grandma and Grandpa,
with teasing uncles at home
from LisaNLori, my cousins within walking distance.

When I peruse the half-finished baby books, the photo albums, the silly writings, and the depths of my soul;
I laugh and ache for where I'm from.

High School's Spontaneous Overflow of Emotions
Recollected in the Tranquil Mind
of a Thirty-Something English Teacher

It's a thousand years to yesterday
to a place I left in order to get there –
From this view there's a laugh under pain
As much as there's always been pain under the laugh

I walk with you wanting to stop you, to be you
Knowing you make the same mistakes
with a remorseful sigh for what you can't change
even though I want to now

Through the halls and the classrooms
 to the delicious hot summer nights on old country roads
 and the fear of what if?
And the should I or shouldn't I? and the no one will ever know . . .
Cheating and singing and laughing and learning the basics: life,
love, lies.

Best friends pledging not to tell the dark secrets;
praying mine are buried deep enough as they surface in you.
With caution and excitement you jump in to my consequences
as I rush to join you, holding you back.

Trying to get to yesterday to keep you from the regrets of
tomorrow
Every day gets a thousand years longer
 and you never learn to do it right
 no matter how many times
 I relive it.

The Opening

```
I am who I've become
not who I was
not who you made me
or who you wanted me to be
But instead
     who I always wished I was
```

The Beginning

Outside the window of my soul
I watch it pour –
 the pain, the fear, that ache in my stomach – the feeling of being about to cry
It won't go away
Like I'm about to vomit
what's left of my soul right out into the world so it's easier to trample that way
With me as the empty shell

Devoid of regret, of memory, of laughter, of joy – of pain. . .
 of sorrow. . .of reality, of hope
But alive and here to serve
To serve my family
In my empty, soul-less shell of what used to be me

As the thunder crashes
& the rain cries the tears of my broken-hearted soul

■■■

An Observation on the Way Home

a cracked marriage is like a cracked windshield
if you don't fix it when its small, it will spread until the whole thing is completely

shattered

Really Trying

It rips at me and tears at me,
an emotionally physical experience of burning my stomach into
nervous knots of
       what I could have,
            should have,
                would have done
       if I'd relived any of those broken moments.

And I read the signs put in front of me about peace
       and finding it in God
            and letting go of the past,
                  not letting it consume you in its fire

and I promise I'm trying
"Be still and know that I am God"
and I promise I'm trying to change and let it go
"Pray without ceasing"
and I hear the Spirit calling
and my soul <u>wants</u> to be ok and know that
"peace, perfect peace"

But it is destroying me
and making me unsure of any real peace
       And as I write, my stomach leaps in nervousness
            feeling it again

this time at writing down my not-so-complimentary thoughts
And I remember the voices saying "You've got to let it go"

But it's there, still, lingering, salivating, preying on my lost & wandering soul

Will the guilt ever leave me alone?

Surely your peace is not like Tylenol
Pray and feel the peace for 6-8 hours at which time you must pray again to relieve the
        pain

■■■

Yesterday was a band-aid
But I have to believe that each day You, my Father, will apply a new band-aid
Until the wound is healed

■■■

It's a never-ending feeling of dread,
still there, lingering,
waiting
        to pounce
                when you think
        everything is going to be ok

Addicted

I'm addicted to you
when I don't have you, I want you

When I do have you, I want more of you

I can't get enough and even if you kill me,
      even if you destroy my dreams,
      even if you cause me physical pain
      when you don't let me have you,

I only ache for more. . .
      and more . . .
           and more. . .
                and more of you.

Until you consume my every thought, and I honestly believe I can't live without you.

if only I'd lose 20 more pounds
if only I'd pray harder and longer
if only I'd make the house spotless
if only I'd iron every piece of clothing
if only I'd hang on his every word
if only I'd keep my mouth shut so he wouldn't have to pause the game
if only I'd write him love poems
if only I'd fix his favorite meals
if only I'd smile when he walks in the door
if only I'd pray harder and longer
if only I'd make sure the kids did chores
if only I'd leave work at work
if only I'd follow him wherever he wants me to be
if only I'd buy him things to boost his spirits
if only I'd pay all the bills and never tell him we have no money
if only I'd write down every day why I love him
if only I'd fix his plate at supper
if only I'd make sure his glass was always full
if only I'd pray harder and longer
if only I'd be better organized
if only I'd cook desserts
if only I'd smell good
if only I'd be irresistible

if only I'd be happy while I do it all
if only I'd keep my thoughts to myself
if only I'd learn to ignore the me inside

everything would be ok?

in memory of. . .

in memory of my youth,
  i played the tapes of our songs today.
in memory of my youth,
  i grasped meaninglessly for your hand.
in memory of my youth,
  i looked deep into your eyes for what was hidden.
in memory of my youth,
  i read the passionate words that you had written.
in memory of my youth,
  i sought beauty, desire, and falling in love .

in memory of my youth,
i buried the last of my fears
        in a crypt of lies and truth
                entangled.

Working Suicide

Sometimes I work
       to avoid killing myself
Take that as you will
But right now I'm at work
Is it necessary?
Is it mandatory?
No, but alone with me is where I want to be
Because alone, I can hurt no one else
       but myself
But I'm working
       to avoid killing myself

my soul is a thousand years old
yet just come to life
It is a piece of You, Oh Lord, a piece of goodness and righteousness
With a hint of Sin erased by Your Son
                                              over and over again
And I fret over forgiveness
And I fret about Sin
I read Your Word with the Spirit's guidance
        To the scriptures I read . . .
                I fret again . . .

Joni says that it's forgiven already – Grace at the Cross

but if I know I'm sinning and sin again,
  beg the Spirit to lead me away from sin

      As my flesh cries for something different

  How far does Grace reach?
  Does it go There?

There's nothing worth losing God's Grace.

Is it possible to be an unhappy Christian?
To feel unfulfilled with what God has blessed you with?

      It is sinful no matter what we *tell* the Spirit.

My soul aches to be right again;
I keep wondering how/where/when/why/how. . . . . .

      Take me now, NO, not You, **not *You***

      Take me now, Father, Son, Spirit . . .
              Renew me in your strength;
                      make me whole

Unspoken

It's what's left hanging there
when you've said what you can
without breaking
It's what you think of later
when you're alone and can think
without wanting
It's what you could never express
when you wanted to
without crying
It's what you bury in that hiding place
when you walk away
without speaking

The Brink

When I stand on the edge of a cliff,
            I am consumed with the urge
                    to plunge forward.

    It is a physical request
        and my mind refuses to comply.

And now I've approached the edge of a cliff
            and am consumed with the urge
                    to plunge forward.

    It is a mental request
        and my physical struggles to
        comply.

It hasn't even been 24 hours,
and I'm already having withdrawals –
I want more,
I feel like I *need* more,
like it's something I can't get through the day without.
I can't think of anything else,
but I just keep repeating it
in my head over and over again:
Your arms
your chest
your smell
your touch
how it felt to have my arms around you
your lips on mine

How can I ever forget?
I can't
It is etched in my mind
my heart
my soul
for all eternity
keeping me under your spell
in your power

I want to be in your thoughts as you are in mine
I want you to hunger
to long for me
like I'm lost longing for you

In love
Your heart beats

You're breathless at his voice

Your thoughts are unfocused

You're thinking only of him

And that moment

Everything changed

With a kiss

How can I show anyone who I am without letting them in?

Stay outside the door and just peek through the window, please.
  Only see what I want you to see.

> The rest is for God.
> He knows it all and swears He loves me anyway.
> He's the only real and perfect love,
>   which is wonderful and scary at the same time.
> It's what we search for in a man.

My friend reminds me how temporary this life is.
I try to hold on to that thought
  and that someday
    I'll be held in the arms of the
      True & Perfect One who knows it all and loves me anyway.

Beautiful
Hott (with 2 t's he says, spell it right for the English teacher)
When I look in the mirror
I try to see the one they describe
But I see me
Less than perfect
Slightly aging
which is, I think,
exactly who you see
If you could see the beautiful me. . .

Muse

I guess I'm a muse of sorts –
inspiring them to write –
to dip deep in their souls
and find the words to express the hole in their hearts

They share with me their words –
        souls on paper
And I do not judge or change
But listen with my soul
                      and hear the depth of their pain
                            and anger
                                    and sadness
                                            and desires
                                                    and love
And only that . . .
        Because changing a soul cannot be done with a red pen
                and a tense correction.

a muzzle
covering my mouth
to keep my thoughts from biting

You'll sing to me love songs and promises made of dust
And I will gather flowers and walk beside the falls
Sing to me of roses and spirits intertwined
I will play your heart strings and love you all day long
Sing to me of princesses and knights of long ago
I'll plant promises in the garden of your soul
Sing to me of beauty unsurpassing and love so strong it never dies
And I'll walk with you in moonlight on the lakeside shore
We'll sing a song for all eternity as we love
      the way that nature does – free and full and true

Peter Part 1

I don't want to live in your pumpkin shell anymore.
A woman is not made to be kept, to be limited.
I want you to love me because you love *me*.
I want to love you because of who you are,

Not because I have to,
    not because the world
        or the church
            or my friends
                or this stupid pumpkin shell demands it.

Peter Part 2

Today
Maybe I <u>do</u> want to stay in your pumpkin shell
Today
I pray to feel satisfied with the pumpkin shell, to expect no more
Today
I think maybe an anti-depressant or maybe just stifling the voice
    will teach me to respect the pumpkin shell,
        where I'm surrounded by security,
        which should be good enough.

I hear the voices all around me saying it will get better
        or it could be worse
And I don't want to be a Job saying what else?
        how could it be worse?
        And then have it thrown at me.

But it's hard to stay positive and happy or even just OK
        when I don't see there being a happy ending
        until I'm in heaven
And the road in-between here and there hardly seems worth it

It's all I can do not to scream.
It's all I can do not to cry.
It's all I can do not to hit.
It's all I can do not to leave.
              to run away as fast as I can
              to just go
              to just go wherever is *away*

And all I can do is pray
And all I can do is cry
And all I can do is be silent

Someday . . .
she'll walk in the door and you'll have to catch your breath

Someday . . .
she'll smile at you from across the room and you'll see no one else

Someday . . .
she'll thank God for the knight in shining armor she sees in you

Someday . . .
she'll pray by your side and hold your hand as you lead her spiritually

Someday . . .
she'll capture your heart in a way you never thought possible

Someday . . .
she'll laugh and you'll do whatever it takes to hear it again and again

Someday . . .
she'll love you for who you are and give herself to you unconditionally in marriage

And you *will* live happily ever after

I won't kill myself.
No guts for that.
Plus, I don't think that's the way I want to go.
Plus, my **faith** won't let me.

So I don't guess I'm suicidal.

That's not to say I don't think about
my death.

That's not to say I don't think about
how badly I wish I was in heaven already.

That's not to say I don't think, every day, about
how the people who try to tell me they'd be affected if I died,
the people who act like they need me,
about how they would be able to move on
and would be happy
and wouldn't have to feel
like they had to reassure me all the time,
wouldn't have to feel
like they had to keep me from killing myself,

which I'm not going to do.

So I don't guess I'm suicidal.

Conflicted

man vs self
internal conflict
character beating herself up
physically
mentally
either one

man vs nature
getting old
fighting the battle to stay young
which leads back
to the internal conflict
of making choices

head vs heart
responsibility vs freedom
reality vs fantasy
truth vs truth

Seduction

Seduce me with your words
Caress my soul, not my flesh
Whisper the words I desire
And feel the pulsing of my heart

    as you seduce me with your words

what is *this* exactly?

it's . .
poetry rebuilt
laughter redefined
heartache reinvented
pain reinstated
love reincarnated
fear re-explained
doors reopened
fire rekindled
soul restored

Appearances

like clothes
we put them on

They hide our flaws
       what we don't want anyone else to see
And sometimes it's only
       late at night
       in the dark
       all alone
              that we take them off

Can t focus
Can t listen
Can t do anything
Can t think
        of anything else
                but you

What do I want?
What do I need?
What am I doing?

I've become someone else,
      found someone I hid long ago
            under responsibility
            under expectations
            under obligation

But that person of long ago is breaking
            through responsibility
            through expectations
            through obligations

And just living, laughing, loving
                        again

I have no right

no right to want you

to smile at me
to focus on me
to spend time with me
to think of me
to take care of me
to talk to me
to write to me
to laugh with me
to want me
to touch me
to spend every minute of your day
having something to do with me

And only me
no one else

But I have no right to want you.
And you *know* that.
I have no right at all.

indecisiveness
weighing on me like something huge, scary, indescribable
unreal

I think

My sister-in-law said, "You're the one who always seemed to have it together." The soccer coach said the same thing.
I think that it's not that I'm different but that those pieces that I covered with masking tape all these years, trying to hold them in the exact right place, the place of perfect teacher, perfect daughter, perfect wife, perfect mother, perfect Christian, perfect friend. . . it's like the tape just started peeling, you know like the paint on your house: it starts in one little spot, and it doesn't look bad, & no one notices it really, but then another piece chips off, and another, and another, until you start seeing more of what's been underneath all along. And no one really says anything because they don't want to be rude, but they all notice. And finally, someone says, "You know, you're beginning to look a little worn." They tell me my outer joy is gone. And then the next person notices, & another, & another, until almost complete strangers are coming up to ask if I'm ok. But by then the coat underneath, the pieces, are falling off, sometimes recoverable, sometimes shattering into a thousand pieces never to be repaired. I'm trying to walk the road everyone suggests – to cover up the paint & start again with something brighter, better than before. And the counselors say that I have to prepare the bottom layer first, coat it with forgiveness, prayer, the steadfast love of the Lord, that I have to scrape off the bad spots, the places that will never look the same again but can still be treated. The paint is there, the paintbrush has been given to me, but I am scared, I'm scared of what I'll find underneath, I'm scared that the layer below has changed shape, that the pieces won't fit, won't fit where they used to fit. I guess I'm just worried that I'll never be the one who has it together again, that I'll always be the house that needs just one more coat, that needs just one more shade to be well, to be whole, to be who God planned me to be. Because I think I picked up a piece along the way that didn't really belong to me in the first place but that I can't shake, that I can't just give to someone else, but that no one will accept in my puzzle, a piece that needs me to just put it back where I found it & leave it alone. So I'm trying; I'm trying to repaint my house, to color it with the expectations of others and become that person, the one everyone thought they knew, the one who had it all together because hiding behind the paint may kill me inside, but at least I'm not an eyesore for everyone else.

huge snowflakes
    falling
        falling
            falling
                falling

                    falling like I fell for you
                            slow, soft, unexpected, beautiful

but melting away --

            impossible to hold onto

where did it begin
the pain, the fear, the desperation
where did it begin
with a kiss, a touch, an "experience"
where did it begin
the guilt, the shame, the desperation
where did it begin
with the first guy, or the second, or whichever one I'm on now
where did it begin
the pleading, the crying, the desperation
where did it begin
with the date, the marriage, the kids
where did it begin
the pain, the fear, the desperation

when will it end?

lexapro, alcohol, even advocare
it's all just artificial joy
try it, though, because it might just get you through life
and the afterlife is what you want anyway

■■

I realize it wasn't the anti-depressant making me better –
    It was you ---

But I guess it's too late now

■■

Goodbye
a loaded word of consequence
Alone
now you're there

Christmas
a time of giving
what if I'm drained?
what if I can give no more?
I see the lights, the trees, the smiles
in other people's houses and I catch my reflection
in their windows and I know it's over –
there's nothing left of my soul
so why fret anymore
about happiness
it's Christmas

Why do we suffer, God?
Why the suffering?
But I know the answer . . .
>   *It inspires poetry.*
Creativity blossoms in an altered state of mind.

If you cannot do drugs, do **life.**

It's a miserable place in which you never learn your lesson
>   and you just keep ruining it
>   over & over again.

You play all the cards wrong until you're left with an empty hand,
>   an empty life,
>   an empty heart,
>   an empty soul . . .
And what really sucks is you deserve it.

You've done nothing to deserve the life you want,
>   or the death you want.
You've done everything to deserve what you got.

So quit crying.
Count your blessings.
And write the damn poetry.

Christmas Eve
white christmas blares at me through the radio
i try to remember the ones i used to know
and i try to retrieve that feeling, to bring it back to the surface
i know that once upon a time the days felt merry and bright
but right now most days feel dark, sad and lost
what i dream of i'll never know
wishing for my youth, for a time I want to try again
christmas cards – hmph—there were none this year
what do you say in this state of mind –
       Greetings from this deep dark hole I've created for myself?
       Happy holidays from a family who is not?

may all your christmases be white . . . .

i make it a day, two, three . . . today's the record . . . four in a row
with no tears, no tightening in my chest and throat . . .
no fear of what i've done before . . . .
no fear of what i'm thinking in my head . . .
no fear of what my heart is doing . . .
but i'm maxed out on that . . . .
and now i'm feeling it all at once . . .

ive decided today
im finished with boys
all of them
all the ones ive loved anyway
im finished with heartbreak
im done with this tightness in my chest
im through with crying myself to sleep
im done
they dont need me
so i wont need them
today thats the plan

of course, if *you* call me tomorrow, i'll answer . . .

tomorrow is the first day of the rest of my life
geez, that seems ridiculous
but tomorrow begins the new year
all these people make resolutions
and promise themselves that this will be the year
im tired of making promises to myself
resolutions
it's all a heap of nothing anyway
just one more way to set myself up for disappointment
im learning that expecting nothing
of myself
or anyone else
keeps me disappointed
and somehow if you are continually in this state of hardness
then your heart cant keep breaking
which is my resolution
or would be, if i believed in making them
but i dont

new year's revolution**

i will be *me*
i will be true to my *heart*
i will follow my *dreams*
i will be **strong**
i will not let you push me down
i will not just let life pass me by
i will *laugh*
i will step **out** of the pain
i will no longer let you bring out the **negative** in me
i will *rest*
i will make *time* for me
i will *find* what i seek
     and if what i seek is separate and apart from what you expect,
          i will seek it anyway
i will no longer live for you
i will *live*

i will have the **courage** to tell you this
i will *speak* out
i will be my own *revolution*

**revolution: a sudden, radical, or complete change

my whole identity is really based on boys. I don't know where to go with that.

■■■

sometimes it's not the fire that we need but the slow, steady heat.
sometimes it's better to be respected than adored.
sometimes it's less confusing to stay than to leave.
sometimes it's harder on your heart to love than it is to stay where it's comfortable.
sometimes it's a friend who shows you the way when you are blind.
sometimes it's not listening to our friends that causes heartbreak.
sometimes love is stronger than heartache.
sometimes heartache is inevitable.
sometimes my heart aches.
sometimes I love . . .

today is a new day
and today I won't be sad anymore
I won't let the tightness in my chest rain from my eyes
I make a vow to put God first in my world
to put my family next
to put my friends and students' needs before my own
I vow to be the person I need to be
rather than the person I could be
And I am promising myself to be happy, to be content, to hold strong
I will not let my thoughts turn away from where they should be
I will not let my thoughts enter the realm of pain or heartache
But I will not let my broken heart heal, either
because it will remind me that my focus is easily tested
but that happiness from an addiction cannot last
because what you are addicted to doesn't need you like you need it
So I will keep my broken heart
but I will not let it pour forth from my eyes anymore
today is a new day

choices

I make them but it doesn't matter
I have no control over my life
It's everyone else's life anyway
I would like to say God is in control,
        that I've turned it over to Him.
But God only has people to work with,
        and they may not let Him control what they say or do
                or *don't* do.
The advice I get is that I should make my own choices,
        that I can choose this path or that path,
            but that's really a falsehood because some paths are
blocked.
Because the path I choose keeps locking me out, what choice do I have?
The open path . . . the less favorable one, but the one where everyone is pushing me.

You see, it's **NOT** my choice.
They've never been my choices; I've always been pushed and shoved here and there.
So, finally, after 31 years, I decided to choose what I wanted,
        to be who I want and with whom I want,
            but that choice *shut the door on me . . . and refused to love me.*
Listen to your heart and follow your heart, they say,
        but that only leads me to the one who denies his heart . . . .
So, the only choice I really have is the only one anyone really makes on her own:
        live a dead life or kill myself.
And because I cannot kill myself, again, I really have no choice.

Today's prayer
                        T r a p p e d
somewhere between where I was
                        and where I'm supposed to be
somewhere between what once was
                        and what is meant to be
somewhere between God's original plan
                        and His new one
And I wait . . . .
                and pray . . .
                and try to figure out exactly what I'm praying for. . .

Only I keep coming back to the realization that I don't know what to pray for . . .
and this time, no matter what anyone tells me,
                        I think that's ok.

Because You, My Father, know what I need, and that's what I pray . . . .
            that You guide my steps . . .
                that You lead me to my decisions . . .
    Sometimes I dwell on the Sin and forget that it's Forgiven . . .
        Because not everyone believes that it is . . .
            But I am listening to You now, God . . .
            and I believe the Sin is Forgiven with the Son . ..
            and I'm listening for the Spirit . . .

You have a Plan, and it has **all** been part of You . . .
        You have carried me when I could not walk . . . .
        You sent angels when I could not hear You . . .
            and one to listen when I could not speak . . .
        You told me I am worthy through their mouths
            when I could not believe. .
        You gave me someone to trust . . .
            and to understand me. . .
                and to remind me of Your Love . . .

When I thought the rain would never stop,
                                    You gave me laughter.

When I needed a hand to hold or arms to embrace me,
                                    You provided it.

What I'm realizing is that it was YOU all along, Lord.

In the deepest, darkest days,
You gave my friends the knowledge that I was sinking,
and they, in turn, held out a rope so I could climb out of the hole.. .

And I'm still climbing, but I see You in it all, Lord.
                I see You again, and I trust You to lead me
                      where I should be,
                      even if it's not necessarily
                            where I want to be,
                                  or where others think I should be . . .

I'm trusting You, Lord, and I will *stay* if You tell me to stay . . .

                and I *will* walk alone if You say . . .

      I will follow You, Lord. . . .

              Just show me *me*, Lord, and pave the way . . .

                        I **will** walk the path.

                You are all I need to be whole . . .

you
i'm thinking about you again today
who am i kidding?
i think about you every day
all the time
i dont even see the point of sleeping
because i only dream of you
not necessarily romantic dreams, either
but you're there
an ever-present part of them
and i wake up, still thinking of you
and i work, still thinking of you
and i do things with my kids,
and i think all the time
    about what if?
    and how would you fit in this picture?
if he and i were not
and you and i were
would everything be ok?
i do not doubt my happiness . . .
would my kids be ok?
would we still do the things we do now?
and how, how would we all be part of their lives?
and how would they handle it?
and do i risk their happiness for my happiness?
or would they be happier?
or at least as happy?
would i be bringing them more blessing
    or less?
and when is God going to answer me?
or was He answering today, when i was fighting with *him*
    on the phone and hung up on him,
    and turned the corner
        to see a huge sign with your name on it?
i laughed.
because irony makes me laugh.
and laughing is good.

I miss you.
I miss your comfort when I feel lost.
I miss smiling from deep in my soul.

■■■

why?
why don't you feel the way I feel?
why don't you ache to hear my voice the way I ache to hear yours?
why don't you think about me the way I think about you?
why don't you cry for me the way I cry for you?
why don't you want to love me the way I want to love you?
why don't you look at me the way I look at you?
why did you even make me love you the way I desperately do?
why didn't you walk away when my heart would have still been strong?
why is it that pain you took away hurt less than the pain you now cause?
why did you heal my heart only to break it?
and why will you never answer me?

Inspired on TAKS day, with the breaking of the seals . . .

She accidentally tore them both, she said.
How true, I thought.
I intended to make them both happy,
but I accidentally tore them both.
It was the math, she said.
How true, I thought.
Two plus another just doesn't add up; it was the math.

I don't know what they'll do, I told her.
How true, I'm thinking.
If ever face to face with the knowledge,
I don't know what they'll do.
You may have to start a new one, I told her.
How true, I'm thinking.
If . . . I might have to start a new life.

But maybe, just maybe,
no one will ever know about my second seal.
Maybe telling about hers is enough.

Knots
A revelation at the end of an odd school year
An ode to my high school advisory regulars

I realize that even though my world may revolve around you,
Your world does **not** revolve around me.
And that was *my* mistake.
In trusting as I could be trusted.
Just another knot, another knot binding me to those whom I should be untied not united.

Another knot
      <u>not</u> what should have been
      <u>not</u> what should be
Knotting my stomach, creating a mass of concrete death.

I ignored all warnings of a tangled mess.
Just trying to stay untied now. . .
Trying to keep slack between me and you,
But finding that I'm getting caught in yesterday's knots

Unable to be free

the last time we touched we were in love
the last time we talked like that we were together
the last time our eyes met was like the first time
the last time you held my hand, i knew it was over
the last time we danced i knew to take a deep breath
        and just move
                and move on . . .

the last dance

at what point do we grow up?
ever?
at what point do crushes not hurt?
at what point do the right people get together?
do only the ones that you don't like, like you?
what's the deal?
and will it ever change?

crush

This is a toast
>> to wasted years
>> to human insanity
>> to places lost inside the soul and spirit
>> to fear unspoken
>> to the strengths and weaknesses of women,
>> so dependent on men
>> for reassurance,
>>> guidance,
>>>> leadership
>> so disappointed
>> in real life,
>> in real consequences
>> in real choices
>>> made in a moment
>> of breathtaking falsity

to the woman who finds at 40 that her husband is not in love with her anymoreand finds at 50 that soul mates are real
to the woman who finds at 18 a painful lesson about men's lack of maturity and commitment
to the woman who spends her whole life waiting for the right guy, only to find she's spent her whole life waiting. . .
to the woman at 23 who realizes that roommates don't make husbands and seeks the passion of real love
to the woman who at 50 realizes her roommate husband has lead a double life and must rebuild 24 years of memory
to the woman who at 60 cares for an ill husband out of a sense of responsibility and commitment to marriage
to the woman who at 30 wakes up with a husband, kids, and a desperate crush that leads her where she never should have been
to the woman of 30 who spends her days and nights with a husband who finally found God
to the woman who realizes at 50 that her husband is right as her physical being crumbles away

Who in the end find themselves not dependent on men but on each other
    with a silent hand on a 70-year-old elbow leading her
        independent self
            to the car after a
                merry mother's meeting
                    on a warm May night

woman toast

Your grace is like a pillow
    waiting to soften the pain
        when I fall off the bed

Your grace is like the rain
    running down the window pane
        washing away the dirt

It's a weird world
        But you make me *normal*
Not the normal of who I really am
        But the normal that is best for the life I live
You take away
        my improper thoughts and feelings, the ones buried
You cover them
        with a layer of complacency
You slow
        the
                roller   coaster
                                      It   is
                                              almost   halted

        Almost

You keep me
        on level ground
You take away
        the giddy butterflies
                          and the horrendous heartache
                              and the flaming guilt
You extinguish
        the excitement
                to a
                      s l o w   b u r n
You give me
        a placid place,

        a place where I can help others,
        a place where I am not sad or afraid or anxious or

                or joyful . . .
                                or real
But you make me *normal*

Ode to the Anti-Depressant

Written in a dorky mood on the way home from soccer practice in my dorky-cool van when two college-aged guys looked my way on their way to the softball field . . .

They stare
I smile
homely or hott?
I pull the mirror down
     and my answer appears
"homely"
Inside I cry
Outside I smile
Because I ache happily
     that I AM
          the windblown soccer mom
        on my way home
             to the box of hamburger helper

    longing for my touch

I'm good

really

Until . . .
   I hear someone mention you
       or
   I read a story or poem
       or
   I dream about your touch
       or
   I smell your cologne
       or
   I remember the taste of your kiss

But

I'm good

really

I wrote you a hundred love poems and prayed for you . . .
and me. . . every night
I saw myself in your arms forever holding tight
I promised you a lifetime of looking in your eyes
I told you that I'd wait until the time was right
And I pictured our souls completely intertwined

But . . .
    God said no,
    reminding me of His will, not mine
    And though it broke my heart to follow,
    you proved your heart was fine
    Now I realize God is my strongest tie
    And I let you go, day after day, a little at a time

stand outside the box and look in --

ok, now, what do you see?

so I peer into the box as a spectator now

and I see how lost I was, I see how disoriented I'd become, and I see that while there were many hands just reaching out to help, that they weren't what I was seeking, that what I was seeking was a past

so I sought it unintentionally, in fact just sort of fell down the rabbit hole of Alice's dream,
and woke up in my past,
giddy with the feeling of first love and youth and that leap at the sound of his voice or the touch of his hand.

but like Alice, I discovered it was *un*reality,
and that sometimes the arms of comfort are waiting to catch us all along, if only we knew which direction to turn,
and it wasn't the funny, crazy characters who lead me home,
but the solid, grounded characters who **are** my home

If God blinked ---
how long would it last and would it be worth it –
to taste sin without fear –
--But then again, if God blinked,
        He would probably prepare the world
            so that the sin I wished would be impossible, you know,
                      unavailable to me in that very moment . . .
and by the time I found it or won it, God's eyes would be opened –
            Just in time to see me sin . . .

                      or maybe He's always blinking . . . .

Inspired by 2nd Timothy 3 and the students that break my heart . . .

      I   AM
Banging my head against a wall
Over and over again, trying   to tell you
                                 to teach you
                                 to guide you
                                 to lead you
Not because I am   a prude
                     or a religious fanatic
                     or a saint

But because if I save you
               I will feel redeemed
                           not that I need to . . .

But because I want to save you
                     from pain
                     and guilt
                     and addiction

And because I know where you are going
     because you're treading my path
        And you're following my heart
        And you are using my justifications

God won't let me let go
   He's taught me   to teach
                     to show others   the guilt
                                               the pain
                                               the addiction

  To save you . . .and him. . .and her . . . whoever
                                               listens
                                             when I yell

And beat my head
                     against the brick wall

The Greatest of These Sestina

Told but not taught how belief is faith,
That the three most important will give you hope,
That when all else is gone, all you need is love
But they don't give you the tools to mold
Your character or instruction on listening to the Spirit,
So your religion fades away and becomes your past.

I watch the children look at me with the eyes of my past.
I approach each lesson for them with the faith
That they can succeed, that their inner spirits
Will guide their quest for knowledge. A teacher's greatest hope
Is that students will learn to love learning, that she can mold
Them into productive citizens, able to fully understand and love.

There is really nothing greater than a mother's love
My children provide a glimpse into the future with a link to the past.
My goal as a parent is to give them experiences that mold
Them into good Christians with a strong enough faith
To see them through life's heartaches and give them hope
That every day will be a blessing for their lively spirits.

There are days when I lack the energetic spirit
Of a servant, days when it is hard to love
Others or myself, days when I think there is no hope,
Days when I worry and fret and dwell on the past,
Days when I hear the Bible speak, "O Ye of little faith,"
Days when dinner is about the only thing I mold.

On those days, I realize that you are the ones who mold
Me, the children who show me your fiery spirits,
Open minds and intelligent thoughts that bring back my faith.
And I'm no longer lost but totally engrossed and in love
With my job and my family and can again see past
All my concerns with a future full of hope.

I seek again my church home and my Bible with renewed hope.
I listen to the songs we sing, asking the Father to make and mold
Me. I find that He completely erased what is past
When He gave to me the joyous gift of the water and the Spirit.
And I know that I must do what He asks and simply love
All I come in contact with and in that, I will have faith.

So I run spiritedly past my fear,
Praying for my faith to mold me,
     Hoping that my love for people is strong enough to give.

Intermediary

Every day you wake up thinking that today is it. Today is the day that is going to be different. Today's the day that guilt won't attack. Today is the day that Satan finds someone else to torment. Today is the day that my heart won't hurt, that the sadness of the past won't find me, won't bring me down. Today is the day that the past is past, that the present is reality, and that reality is good. Today is the day that will be better than yesterday. Today is the day the lump in my throat and the heaviness in my chest will be gone. Today is the day that I begin again.

And it is. But what you realize is that today is every day. And that every day, you are faced with the reminders, the triggers, Satan's photographs of you in your mind, that even with the joy of the Lord in your soul and in your heart, that even when you erase mistakes, it leaves residue, and that the residue is real, too. And you long for what you hate. And you hate what you long for. So you take that and you run with it and know that God wants you to pray. So you pray, you pray for the pain of loss, you pray for the people that you know are aching, the ones who can still make the best choices, and for the ones who didn't. You pray for the people who hurt you most. You pray for the ones who make you angriest. And you spend every waking hour of prayer earnestly praying for your true love, the one who promised to grow old with you, the one who warms you every night and gives you strength and wisdom and challenges you and brings you back when you go too far and sends you out when you stay too long. And you know in your soul that today is every day and that every day is a new day in your commitment and your journey and your growth. And you smile through the tears, and you know love.

It's like

                        stepping off into space
                        leaping through time

     adrenaline pumps

                    through my soul

                                and my body

wet
  warm
    soft . . . and rough
      rich
        sighing into it

one timeless action

                            committing our live and hearts,
bodies and souls

                      to intimacy

all else fades to nothingness

                  when we kiss

depression too

It's a funny thing about depression
You think you're good
That you'd be better off the meds

And then something like a lost remote or no-clean sippy cups or catching the last minute
                of some show you've seen before

Sets you off

And you get that "oh crap I'm about to cry" feeling or like you're about to throw up,

and

Somehow feeling that feels good
  because at least you feel something that feels real.

Today's the day I step out there.
I put it all on the line.
I say, here I am, lost, afraid, confused by the thousand voices of
reason floating around and in my head.
I lay it down in front of you.
I tell you that I trust you, and I step over the edge into the abyss . . .
I am falling, falling so fast that my heart is pounding,
my insides flutter . . .
I tell you everything I feel without holding back, without stopping
myself.
And I keep falling, falling . . .
For your voice
and your touch
and your words
and your heart

And I wonder will you really protect me?
Are you falling with me? Or are you just pushing me?
Are you afraid?

But, here I am, waiting, waiting, waiting . . .
For you to reassure me
to protect me
to tell me everything I want to hear
to promise
        that you aren't pushing me out to be beaten *by* the others,
              like the others have done
but that you are falling with me, reaching out for my hand
              at the same time

        I reach for yours.

FICTION

He stepped into the room and woke her up from the dream that had become her life. She thought it was the way she wanted; it was everything she had always planned. It had all happened the way she planned. But feelings aren't planned. And romance is not tomorrow's reality when you pick the wrong soul for the dream. She tried to fix it, to control it, to make it good and make him well and make him the person she thought he could be. But she realized the romance wasn't real; it was a lost cause of unhappiness.

So when he walked in with his smile that made her heart leap and his words that were so perfect, so full of romance, she had no choice but to finally wake up. And that's what she did. She stepped out of the pain.

He held out his hand to pull her through. He wrote her love poems and gave her his soul every day. He kissed her with passion every morning when they woke up and every night before they went to bed and sometimes in between just to see her smile. And she did smile. She smiled and laughed and she found who she really was deep in her soul; she found that person she had buried with perfection. And by doing so, she became his perfect soul mate, and he became hers.

But what if he never stepped in the room? Or what if he takes the first door out?

If money can't buy happiness
And eating to be happy isn't healthy

And obviously, searching sin for happiness is wrong,

Then is it wrong to be happy?

Should we all be praying for misery?
Or is it that when we can't find happiness,
      we realize that we *were* happy
      when we thought we weren't
Which is really quite ironic and sad if you think about it,
Which you really shouldn't do
because thinking doesn't bring happiness either

Just move

Take a day at a time

Take a cup of joy instead of reaching for the whole pitcher

prom date

just step back into the shell and breathe
who cares
no one has to like you
you do not have to be who you cannot be
breathe, breathe, breathe
you are not her
you must go in the shell
just stay there, in your shell
let the world happen around you
while you sit
inside yourself
let them ask you questions
give them the answers he wants to hear
give them the answers he expects you to have
just answer briefly with your wifely smile
and your devoted comments about him
and your praise for what a wonderful person he is
and what a wonderful school it is
and just stay in your shell, knowing that you are your own worst enemy
you can ruin everything if you don't stay there
just stay in the shell
stay in the shell and breathe
and smile and pass the perfection quota
you can do it
no one has to like you
they have to like him
you have to be her
you can be her
just stay in your shell and breathe
give them what he needs
because it is time you make a habit of that

of burying her inside the shell
because it is the only way you will live

weather the storm

it's what I do

but some days I begin to erode
some days im not so good at weathering
some days its easier to just let the water o'ertake me
some days I no longer want to fight

some days I'm so angry at myself that I can't wake up
some days im not fair to anyone else
some days I just really want to just be buried in me

Grief
It comes when we least expect it
Burrowing a hole in the soul
And welling up with overflow
Until that punch in the stomach
 and drop of the heart
Makes you feel like you can no longer stop
  the crack in the dam
Because it is no longer one burrowed hole in the dam
But a break
a catastrophic split of your spirit
Pouring out through the water well of your eyes
And just when you think it's over
It starts again, with a new catalyst of tears streaming hotly down your cheeks
And deepening the crevice in your heart
and the hole in your soul
Eroding any relationship that gets in its way

Sunday school
they bring us in, look us over, ask where we're from, where we've been, and we hide and smile
we give them the sunday school answers, the churched response, the "family with-it-all-together" faces
we mask our grievances and lie our griefs; we hide the scars behind the petty words of what we do for a living and where we live and the surface reason why we moved
we're on the firing range, the altar, waiting to be unclothed, revealed for what we are, which is battle-sore, weary, broken and tired and longing for someone to see
to notice that we need a home, a place with acceptance and insistence in making us accountable
and we don't **want** anyone to know what was covered by grace, but we **need** everyone to know what was covered by grace so that they are able to really see us, to really guide us, to really know us and support us and give us strength when we're weak
to hold our feet to the fire when they see us walking on coals and dipping our thoughts into the soup of regret
but what do you say?
here we are, imperfect, at times a little insane, sad, and angry with each other, full of counseling we sometimes forget how to use, slipping some days into patterns of the past, desperate for someone to remind us how to live through Christ.
and let them line us up and walk away?

Mr. Rogers says, "Who we are in the present includes who we were in the past."
Why is that concept so hard to accept? Why do we want to change the past, to rewrite who we were – is it to change who we are? Yes, that's it. We are unhappy with who we are, so we want to change what we did before. If only I had done this or hadn't done that, I would be so different, and everyone would love me. Or would they? Because I wouldn't be me. Embrace the mistakes; embrace the past – consider that your present .

Every day we bring up old wounds; we dredge through muddied waters we can't seem to clean. We take a step out of the darkness into the light and then slip four more steps behind, forgetting what we learned yesterday about ourselves. If we are lucky, there is someone there to catch us before we fall again, someone to remind us which path is best, which way is less entangled with death. If we are lucky, circumstances will present themselves, tests that we can pass, days that we can say we have grown. If we are lucky, these events, these people, will occur often enough that we won't lose our footing completely, that we won't step out on the balcony again, ready to jump, to leap forward into an abyss of strangeness, of stupidity, to step on the crumbling mass below and fall into the welcoming arms of disaster.

heard jon bon jovi on the radio
thought of the you I used to know
stayin' 16 is an impossible dream
but I'm still hangin' on to the young you & me
talkin' on the phone 'til late at night
writin' love letters to make up a fight
knowin' you were the one meant for me
and tryin' so hard to make you see

with your smile and your kiss and your sweet, loving hands
you're all I need
not a day that goes by that I don't wonder why
we can't be
everything we were back then

your eyes, they would melt me with their sea of blue
holdin' hands and maybe sneakin' a kiss or two
hearin' a song that was sung just for us
laughin' and cryin' and sharing so much
talkin' 'bout the future and where we'd be
when we were old enough to make everyone see

that your smile and your kiss and your sweet, loving hands
were all for me
not a day that goes by that I don't wonder why
we can't be
everything we were back then

now the past is the past
and there's no turning back
so I try & remember when
your smile and your kiss and your sweet, loving hands
were all I'd need
not a day that goes by that I don't really try
to make you see
your smile and your kiss and your sweet, loving hands
breathe life into me

babe, you're all I need

sometimes I travel to the lost little recesses of my mind, the places no one else sees, no one else is aware of. sometimes I go there to find answers, sometimes I go there to escape, sometimes I find peace and solace there and sometimes I only find more questions. sometimes I remember when I go there and sometimes I go there simply to forget what is going on. sometimes I truly believe that I can change myself and sometimes I truly believe that I can change everything around me, who surrounds me, who possesses my time and thoughts, who controls me.

You shut that door in your mind,
lock it with chains of regret,
bolts of forgiveness,
nail it with faith, prayer, scripture, and common sense.
And you seal the windows with distance.
And you breathe from deep in the soul,
to stay focused.

But sometimes it feels like the only thing holding the door shut is you
pushing as hard as you can with everything you have,
struggling to keep it closed
because it would be easier
to just let go.

your part in my story is over now.
the page has turned, the new chapter has begun
you changed your setting and I changed mine
your part is over now
the weight of the whys and hows and the what was I thinking? will no longer hold me down
the wait of the when and the if and the fear of the publication will no longer hold me down
your part is over now
the conflict of who and soul mates and romance and love has been resolved
the inner conflict of the guilt and the shame and the wishing for something more has been resolved
your part is over now
my character remains – a little tarnished in the world – but still strong in my faith
your character is no longer in my story – you are static, never changing, never moving forward
because
your part is over now
my point of view has changed – I am a new creation in Christ whose mercy and grace forgave me
my point of view is refreshed with the romance of my Lord
your part is over now
learning hasn't been easy and it hasn't been fun, but I have learned the lesson
the theme of leaning on Jesus, of trusting in Him always, of recognizing my weaknesses
like you
but your part is over now
and *my* story goes on

Today's Reality

Sometimes we have to wake up to the reality that reality is already here.

We've stepped on the pebbles and rocks of the path that lead us here, that gave us the calluses on our feet, and we survived, scarred, war-torn, hungry for our Lord and Savior . . . .

The reality is that we make mistakes, life-altering mistakes. Sometimes we can hide behind our secret veils, the masks of our false reality.

But we all sin. We all suffer from guilt and shame. We make choices every day that lead us closer to God and away from God. We make choices that make our reality a little more hidden, a little more painful, a little more frightening. And we make choices that reveal pieces of our souls, that let the light of grace in. Sometimes our pain is eased today; sometimes it seems to take forever to feel the ease.

But the Lord will feel and fill our hunger. He is our rescuer, the knight in shining armor we ask for.

The reality is that today's choices are just that: today's choices.

Exhaustion. . .

Defeat. . .
    Satan's playthings

D r o p p i n g
        down the rabbit hole again,
not the same this time
this time more aware but no less lost,
    no less defeated

It's just that there's no way out
   I tried that door. . . .
and *that* one . . .
and then ran somewhere else to a different door. . . .

None of them took me anywhere except
        back **down**
            into the
                same **dark** place.

everything I do is because of it
everything I say
　　　or write
　　　or give
Or do . . . .
　　　　　　everything is because
　　　　　　　　of that
　　　　　　　　　　one
　　　　　　　　　　　　　desperate
　　　　　　　sad Hope

　　　　　　　Desperately
　　　　　　　　sadly
　　　　　　　　pitifully
　　　　　　　　insanely
　　　　　　Wishing to be loved

Unloved
What I feel when I'm alone
    and lonely
When he is working
    and no one will answer me
When he is home
    and yelling at me
When I sit by myself
    in the pew
Wishing the preacher wasn't
    preaching to me
When I try too hard
    to be loved

It's what I feel
Unloved

Broken-hearted
again and again
if only i could harden my heart
if only i didn't need to feel loved
Hating my world

I'm laughing at weirdness today. . .
like irony in unexpected places. . . .
like the way the corrupted files throw words into my poetry . . .
like the word "normal" thrown in . . . .
like thinking about what exactly is my "default" personality . . .
and is it faulted . . . flawed . . . .unacceptable . . . .???

In the bottom of the barrel
      my reflection *lies*
        and stares me straight into the darkness
In the bottom of the bottle
      my fear resides
        and beckons me to throw away the light

I am **not** a Barbie
Not plastically perfect
Time has given me the gift of padding
So that when I run into things, my parts don't crack and break off
You can't color on me and wipe it off – the words you color *stay*
But my hair *will* grow back if you cut it
Which gives me an advantage over Barbie
And when I stand, it is not **always** on my tip-toes –
 although I seem to walk around a lot like that at home
My eyes are **not** a perfect blue or green or even brown
          but a mixed-up conglomerate of each
I do **not** smile *all the time*
    nor do I want to
A plastic soul-less empty shell-
She smiles at Ken and rocks his world
    on her tiptoes *all the time*
Destined to fall forward before gravity takes effect
    on her massively disproportionate chest
I am **not** Barbie
I am flawed
But my soul is **real**,

    . . . and I bet I could lure Ken away anyway –
                     if I really wanted to

When again I glimpse your words,
        a smile, a tear, a memory . . . I hold dear.
Inside my world there's no longer room.
I've made my peace and moved along.

But when I reach for you again, with familiarity we speak.
. .
I can remember when you frustrated me,
              when you excited me,
                      when you inspired me,
                            when you gave
meaning to life.
I let you go,
        knowing it was best,
            knowing someday we could be
together again,
                knowing I could take a small
piece of you with me.

But I still long for you sometimes.
        I miss you every day.
            And I will always love you.

A Love Poem for English – (not the language but the subject☺)

Crashing in like tidal waves at sea,

my thoughts, my feelings that won't leave.

Best to forget, to take the road ahead

as I toss and turn lying in my bed.

It's strange how quickly I seem to fall,

  with God, with you – I could lose it all.

And I only wander where I'm lead,

wondering why I keep lying in my bed.

Turning out the light,

 I close my eyes and find you again by my side.

I can feel your breath, your tender touch,

trying to forget, trying to remember so much.

Drifting away with a smile on my face,

 I know these are memories I cannot erase.

And then I awake to hands touching me,

and I remember the place where I have to be.

Tonight I will play the memory again in my mind

and then play the part for which I am destined.

I will even convince my own heart and head, tonight,

 of the reason I'm lying in my bed.

ok. so I walk out and then what.
I pick up the pieces.
I send myself a letter about how I'm going to be ok. I remind myself with greeting cards and sing-alongs. I give myself the encouragement I need and satisfy my needs with whatever is on hand.
I must first lose myself to find myself. that's what they all say but I write with desperate feeling now begging someone to answer me when I cry out to protect me when I'm weak to shelter me from the storm. only you, oh god, can do that. my constant begging for someone here to do that has gotten me nothing but disappointed. I've spent every year every month every day every minute every second lost in what should have been real and wasn't. and now it is time to admit what is real. I am an ok person. I make people laugh. I bring joy to others. I am considerate of others' feelings and compassionate to those who are suffering. I find ways to take care of people who need it. I am generous and forgiving. I have good qualities. I am loyal to my friends. I can keep secrets. I love people. I am a writer. I write well.

the blue colored glass of tomorrow beckons through the gray world and I must find the courage to put my hand through the glass to get there.

in love
we throw it around like a blanket,
> well-worn to the point that it covers everything
and covers nothing
we claim to be in love with food, in love with actors, in love with our own images
but in love is so much more than that
it **is** the food
it is an image, a thought, a devotion, a physical reaction to life
to its limitless boundaries
that seem so real, so perfect, so all-encompassing
when we are truly
in love

9-29-2008 after reading a post on an alzheimers board about being in love . . .

I spent the night in your arms
  wishing away the past
I nestled in to feel your touch
  reaching deep to my lost soul
I felt your lips and touched your skin
  embracing your sweet scent
I heard your voice and saw you smile
  engulfing me in your love

but Dawn peeked through my still shut shades
and beckoned me to come
        and so I left you once again
                and woke up all alone

Xanadu

What my mother taught me

My mother taught me to be on time
to be responsible
that the world didn't revolve around me
that I was smarter than the average person
she taught me
that stupidity is worse than heathenness
that it matters what you look like
that it's ok to rebel if the person in authority has no business being there
that you stay within the parameters where you are untouchable
      by doing a good job
she taught me
that saying "I love you" is trite
that expecting affection somehow connotes inferiority
that accepting others is important, unless it's your own family
she taught me
to wait for sex until marriage
to appreciate Broadway show tunes
to respect my grandma and her generation
to love reading
she taught me
how to kill (or entertain) with sarcasm
how to write effectively
how to shop
how to orchestrate an elaborate birthday party
she taught me
that I couldn't be trusted
that I couldn't talk to her about boys
that having feelings was selfish and ignorant
that she loved me even when she was disappointed
she taught me
how to flirt (not that I needed any lessons)
how to show kindness and compassion to others

how to work hard
how to play board games
how **not** to play sports
how to be critical of others
she taught me
to leave her alone when she had a headache
to sneak around if I didn't want to do what she said
to have my own thoughts
to be independent
she taught me so many things, good and bad, that shaped who I've become
she taught me that I was always and never good enough, and I believed her
I became that person who is always and never good enough for my husband
But I am good enough
I've always been good enough
Her Alzheimer's taught me that sometimes what we expect of our lives doesn't change what happens
So despite the expectations that I'm not good enough, I am
And I forgive her for not teaching me that
Because, actually, I'm **that** good

Not Ready Yet

How many times have I spoken the words, "It's not ready yet" when my kids have asked me about supper or dessert or even when they've needed socks out of the dryer? "Leave it alone. Let it go a little longer. It's not ready yet." When my 11-year-old son asks why he can't have a cell phone, I automatically respond, "You're not ready for that yet."
When my eight year old wanted to walk home from school alone, I told him, "I just don't think you're ready yet." When the five year old asks if he's old enough yet to have a girlfriend, my voice hides the scream inside when I say, "You aren't ready for that yet, son."
It's always so hard to wait for something to be ready. When I was pregnant and the older boys wanted the baby to come but he wasn't ready yet, their anticipation (and mine) seemed almost unbearable. But, obviously, it is better to wait for the right time.
When the cake smell is overwhelming and all you want is a bite, it is a much better reward to wait until it is done than to eat a half-cooked cake.
I know there have been times when I was so hungry that as soon as something was done enough, I'd grab a bite, not waiting for it to cool. While it may have been done, it wasn't ready for me to eat. Consequently, I would burn the top of my mouth and have a constant reminder of how my eagerness can harm me.
Today, I asked God to please just change the circumstances in my life, to give me a husband who treats me like I long for, to rearrange my life somehow. And I heard Him say to me those words I've used so many times before, "You aren't ready yet."
I think of the times I've tried to control my circumstances to get the desires of my heart, only to experience the agonizing

pain like the burn on the roof of my mouth, the kind that fades but not without scraping a part of you first.
I'm not ready yet, He says. So I must put my trust in Him as I continue my journey of self-discovery, of loving who I am in spite of my perceptions, and someday I will be ready. And I know that when I'm ready, it will taste even better than if I tried it too soon.

My Security Blanket

Looking for security I find it in unrest, in disputes, in constant fear.
I tire of it. I want to throw it away, to find a new one.
But even when I try a different blanket, it's not the same. It's not my security blanket.
I try to cover it sometimes, to patch it with prayer.
But even patches can't cover what's underneath.
My security lies in knowing I'm never as good as I want to be, in disappointment and distrust.
It is tattered and used and looks like a mess to the outside, but I'm accustomed to it.
And I'm scared of life without it.

Vomiting Truth

there are days when truth spews from my mouth like vomit
that I can't control, full of chunks of infidelity and immorality
sometimes I try to hold it back, to put my hand over my mouth
but it's like I've developed bulimia,
    like the only thing that will make me feel in control
        is to spew forth the mistakes I make
            to expose everyone to the stench of my addiction
and I never realize it's impact until I see its mess in my life
                      and taste its bitterness.

Steady even sure
your hands lead me
to where I asked to go

Irony rains
    down
        into the hold of depression
to make me laugh
      it's the sign on the street
      or the song on the radio
      or the storm outside the window
          as the storm inside brews
Irony reigns

my heart breaks
    every time he ridicules me
my heart breaks
    every time they draw me in
my heart breaks
    every time a friend turns away
my heart breaks
    every time my mother's disease takes another piece of my
    mom
my heart breaks
    every time I realize my wasted potential
my heart breaks
    every time I look at the future
my heart breaks
    every time my children turn hurt to anger
my heart breaks
    every time my friends hold my hand
my heart breaks
        and breaks
            and breaks
                and breaks

                        beats
            and   on

Leapt in the rain
Nothing on
Bare
Exposed
Refreshed
Desperate
Strong again
Free
New
Blessed by Grace

Inner dialogue

It's that one,
that face that gives you wrinkles
So? So stop.
Stop being annoyed.
They're getting deeper as we speak.
Turning from cracks to crevices. . .
Crevices of anxiety,
depression,
and teaching
idiotic high schoolers.

My feet don't touch the ground
I'm not flying; I'm sitting
But my feet don't touch the ground
There's nothing below to hold them up
They dangle there
Wishing for something to touch
Kicking, swinging
Yeah, that's it – swinging
Searching, waiting to find
Something to reach

Fighting you is overwhelming

There are days I try to combat you and days

I just let you have your way with me

That I just lean into your familiarity

Embrace the feeling

Let you wrap your tight grasp around me

Crushing me inside

Gnawing through my heart

Leaving your path of destruction

buried inside that darkest part of my soul

Waiting, just waiting, for rescue

Will anyone rescue me?

Does anyone believe I'm worth saving?

Does anyone really want to love me?

Is there anyone who will listen?

Anyone who will understand? protect me?

Anyone who will laugh with me?

Anyone who will stay?

Ticking, ticking
    like a clock reminding me of the wasted hours
    or like a bomb just waiting to go off
        to explode and destroy everything around it
    or like my heart,
        speeding up with fear,
            fear of the known
            and fear of the unknown
        wondering which one is better to be afraid of

My heroin, not a heroine,

Nor a hero, though I made him that way in my mind.
But, no, my heroin is not a drug
Yet just as addictive,
Just as destructive,
Just as manipulative and persuasive.
Even when he doesn't call out to me,
I hear him.
I know the promises he makes,
and I remember how it felt to be strung out
Equally destroying as mesmerizing
Killing me just the same

My Quilt
It's pieces of reality
        cushioned with fiction
the pieces alone are rough and shocking
but when I blend them with the untruth
they become softer
a safer blanket to show the world

never driving a sports car
never living in a big house
never having the perfect furniture
never getting flowers for no reason
never opening the surprise jewelry
never hearing someone call just to hear my voice
never being kissed, being held
never holding hands without sex
never having someone in love with me
never being the stay-at-home mom
never keeping a wonderful house
never having the latest gadgets
never dating or partying with friends
never writing my own book

someday has become never

She writes her songs
She writes her heart
She writes the soul she can't impart

She loses strength
when nothing's found
And beats her brain
to higher ground

She laughs at peace
and scorns relief
And curses her eyes
that well with grief

She tries to find a sudden healing
and realizes the pain's not worth concealing

She writes her words and plays her song
And prays each day won't go wrong

I lock him out; I chain the door; I will be safe.
I have turned the light on
and written your words on the walls so I can see.
I fill every fiber of my being with it
 so that it will ooze from my pores.
I try to clothe myself in it,
to see your words every time my eyes close.
I want to bathe in it, to drink it, to be so a part of it that he can
never penetrate my heart or my mind.

But some days it seems like it's not enough,
like when you step outside on a sunny day
and realize there's a north wind
and you don't have enough layers.

He torches the lock and the chains
or he slithers in through the crack I missed.
But I am steadfast and determined this time;
I am steadfast and determined,
and I cling to your words and will not let his darkness in.
He grips at my weakness, tugs at my fears, fills me with tears, and
then punches with the message.
But I will not let him: I look to my wall and I see your words
"Everyone who calls the name of the LORD will be saved."
And I ask Jesus to lock him out this time and chain the door
And I will be safe.

Broken heart

Real, physical pain

Not just a mental mood

Real, real physical pain

Weird, different

In my chest

Tightening

Gripping like a fist

Enclosing my actual heart

It is not detectable by tests

But it is real

Real

Encasing my thoughts

Until I am no longer

Real

Picking up the pieces. . .

Angry words, yelling, ugly, angry words

Then the sound of shattering glass

And the crying and the pleas, "I'm sorry. I'm sorry. Daddy, please."

Shards of glass cover the carpet

Still yelling, he's picking up the big pieces

Leaving the smaller shards

for me, for me to pick up

after he walks away

Still yelling, still screaming, still threatening

To leave

While I continue to pick up the tiny fragments,

the broken pieces that can never be repaired.

Outside the window of my soul
I watch it pour
the pain
the fear
that ache in my stomach
the feeling of being about to cry

It won't go away
Like I'm about to vomit
what's left of my soul right out into the world
so it's easier to trample that way

With me as the empty shell
devoid of regret
of memory
of laughter
of joy
of pain
of sorrow
of reality
of hope
But alive and here to serve
To serve my family
in my empty, soul-less shell
of what used to be me

As the thunder crashes
And the rain cries the tears
of my broken-hearted soul

Someday I'll hear the alarm and listen

I'll wake up and be ready

Today is not the day

Today is the day I get back in line to stay

An eternity spent somewhere in the middle

Not ready to go

Not ready to stay

Just waiting for someone to force me into the right decision

Not stagnant, the line moves

I'm happily chatting at the back, enjoying my time there

When Wham! An explosion shoves me forward to the front –

To the check-out counter

And every time I get there,

It's hard for me to be comfortable with being back in line.

She's new today

Walking through the door

Searching for the promises her grandma sang about standing on

Her heart beckoning, crying out for truth and justice

Even if it brings her to her knees

Lost in her shell, with the plastic smile
  and the hardening of her personality

She's buried alive and begging for answers

But not willing to crack the surface

Too scared to crack the egg of change

Begging God to make her change,
  to force her with redemption

Into not being afraid to be her,
  to be wholly her.

200 years later

I realized who I was

And by then it was too late

Because where I wanted to fit

Where I desperately wanted to be

Didn't fit me

Running hard, running fast
to get ahead, to catch up
Forgetting to breathe
Can't take the time to stop for anything else on the way
Have to keep pushing, keep pressing to get farther down the road

Bittersweet

The taste of finding success in your fear
and finding fear in your success
Sharing hope in your sadness
and sorrow in the hope
The ache of loss in tomorrow's joy
and seeking joy in today's ache
Spending time with your loved one
and your loved one's time spending fast

Nothing more than a smile through the pain
Nothing more to give but back to give again
Pouring out nothing in a world full of sin
In people who don't even know where I've been
Lie after lie sinking deeper from fear

The tears aren't in my eyes anymore
The sadness no longer falls down my cheeks
It stays tightly compressed in my chest
Tightly squeezing
Sometimes a flutter, no, more than a flutter –
    a banging in my chest
   Trying, dying to get out

But I take my imaginary fist and I shove,
     Shove it back down
     Back down as deep as I can
     Deep in my soul
     Farther and farther
     Deeper, deeper
     Bury it
     Bury it

Intermission

Finale

Beaten down

Suffocated
Broken
Rinse with forgiveness
Repeat
Lost
Buried
Muted
Rinse with shame
Repeat
Hidden
Transformed
Stifled
Rinse with fear
No
No more
No shame
No fear
Nothing holding me back
Free to fulfill a dream
Breathing again
Uncaged and unleashed
Finally
Finally found
My Voice

Post- humously: Embracing my broken

Alone with my thoughts
Vulnerability turns to anxiety
Alone with my thoughts
Replaying over and over in my head
Alone with my thoughts
Analyzing each word I've written
Alone with my thoughts
Questioning what I mean to you
Alone with my thoughts
Running round and round my head

Until Now . . .

For years I tried
To find the fix to my broken
In boys and men
In books and stories in my head
In goals and ambitions
In working harder
In humor and sarcasm
In God, Jesus, the Spirit
In counseling, and marriage,
and marriage counseling
In my children
In food – more of it/less of it/more
In saving other people's children
In more counseling
In more boys and men
In a million almost-divorces
In my career
In my Bible as I read every word
In my friends and their stories
In writing and sharing it
In more counseling
In finding the cause of my broken
In filling the cracks and the crevices with things, with sex, with food, with Bible studies and prayer

Yet, in all that time, it never occurred to me (or anyone else) that maybe I just wasn't broken

Until now

I'm beginning to think that maybe my brokenness is the greatest part of me, the greatest piece I have to offer
Maybe, in fact, it's my greatest blessing
And it doesn't need to be filled but accepted, embraced, nurtured, and shared
And desperately loved
By me

Fantasy

I miss the lips I've never kissed
I miss the laughs I've never heard
I miss the hugs I've never felt
I miss the hands I've never held

The heart that never beat beneath my ear
The fingertips that never wiped my tears

I miss. . .
The warmth of your skin
The taste of your tongue
The scent that is only yours
The look in your eyes that is only mine
The sound of your voice whispering my name

And yet my heart flutters
At your words
And the butterflies dance
When I see your face

And my love runs deeper
with each passing day

Ignored
Or beaten down
On edge
Waiting
Lonely
Or frightened
Heart crushing
Either way

Too close to the edge
Fear and excitement mingle
Unknown beyond
I've stepped off before
Only to plummet to a certain end, to a flatline
Leaning over the edge, I try to see the distance,
to sense the Peace and Joy there
While I cling to the ground,
my bare toes like claws
hanging on
To safety
If I just close my eyes and let go . . .
Maybe this time I won't break

Parched
A dry sponge
Wanting
Needing
Just a drop
It satisfies for the moment
Quenches just enough
But the arid atmosphere
Dries it quickly
Parched
Waiting
Longing to be
Saturated

From the Archives

9-12-2005 – actually written a long time ago . . . .

it scares me sometimes
so I try to relate
but I don't understand
why you make me wait
If I get upset over my parents or friends
I call and they say " I don't know when he'll be in"
When everything's going just as it should
Something clicks and it's no longer good
I try to hold on and love you always
cuz I know I've don't things wrong in past days
but I need someone to lift me when I'm down
and never leave – no matter who comes around
I hope someday I'll get what I need
And I hope it's you that does the deed

Ami Part II
We sat at another shower, visiting with old friends.
She, with her degree and job, and me, still in school.
she, talking about going back to England again.
and me, thinking I was probably pregnant.
She, wanting to travel all over the world.
And me, planning to build a house where I am.
And as we left, she again got into her sports car.
And I climbed into my car with the broken steering wheel and
Lost Rearview Mirror

the stable forces of nature
Inside is the award winning horse
Needing a little shine and then galloping away
Right next to the unbroken horse who neighs through the night
despite the pleas to stop Next to him – the timid horse, needing just
an extra round in the ring before riding out into the word.
and in the corner stall stands the long shot whose mane and coat
are tattered and whose dreams are stifled And who, with just a
little care, hope, and faith, can find his gait among the galloping
around him